Fun Stuff With Your Best Friend

—

The Interactive Dog Book

By Nancy Furstinger

Doral Publishing, Inc.
Sun City, Arizona

Doral Publishing, Inc.
10451 Palmeras Drive, Suite 225
Sun City, AZ 85373
1-800-633-5385
http://www.doralpub.com

Printed in the United States of America.

Edited by Mark Anderson
Cover design by Michelle O'Hagan
Interior layout by Mark Anderson

Furstinger, Nancy
        Fun stuff with your best friend : the
    interactive dog book / Nancy Furstinger ;
    illustrator, Bob Ebdon ; edited by Mark Anderson.
    -- 1st ed.
        p. cm.
        Includes index.
        LCCN: 00-10075
        ISBN: 0-944875-66-1

        1. Games for dogs- -Juvenile literature.
    2. Dogs- -Training- -Juvenile literature. I. Ebdon,
    Bob. II. Anderson, Mark. III. Title.

    SF427.45.F87 2000   636.7'0887
                        QBI00-494

In memory of my mother, Helena,
whose smile illuminates moonbeams.

In honor of my father, Frank,
whose dancing feet keep his spirit young.

In praise of their childhood dogs:
Rocky, Sandy, and Queenie.

Table of Contents

Foreword 7

Before You Begin 9

Understanding Your Dog 11

Pethouse 17

Pawsitive Obedience 101 23

Bonding with Bowser 31

Games Dogs Play 39

Frisbee and Flyball 43

Tricks for Treats 49

Clever Canine Tests 55

Bow-Wow Birthday Fun 59

Mutt Makeovers 63

Pampering Your Pooch 69

Seasonal Care Tips 75

Starting a Dog Club 85

A Note to Parents 89

Personalized Pet Pages 91

Further Reading & Information 93

Index 95

Foreword

I've been fascinated by dogs ever since I can remember. Practically the first word out of my mouth was "dog" and as soon as I could string words together, I began pestering my parents for a pooch. Persistence paid off. For my tenth birthday I was given Pretzel—a Wire-haired Fox Terrier.

I've been sharing dreams, journeys, and spontaneous kisses with pooches ever since. I naturally seem to attract dogs—a wonderful thing in my estimation. When I was a toddler, I liked nothing better than to hug every dog I came across. Most of them were much larger than me! Luckily they were all friendly.

Now I enjoy having a steady stream of neighborhood dogs follow Diamond and me on our daily walks. In return, they've helped test market all the recipes in this book. These dogs are convinced I'm the pied piper of canines.

Being passionate about dogs, I enrolled in a professional dog grooming school. The four-legged clients who scampered into my grooming gallery, Barkingham Palace, were lavished with love and individualized attention.

I've discovered that all dogs have plenty to contribute, if only you value their wisdom. Pretzel, my inseparable pal, revealed the joys of wandering. Jazmine's zest for life and melodic howls were contagious. Ariel, who crossed over the Rainbow Bridge too soon, lavished me with unselfish friendship. Sasha Starfoot, my angel and Frisbee-retrieving champion *extraordinaire*, shared her happy spirit with me. Diamond Dreamer, with her tireless tick-tock tail and winking amber eyes, teaches me how to enjoy today's sunshine.

Dogs are my wizards of mirth and I hope that they'll become yours, too. I know that if I had a tail, I'm positive it would be wagging just as happily!

Before You Begin

"The dog was created especially for children.
He is the god of frolic."
—Henry Ward Beecher

Dogs were custom built to play with kids. But sometimes you and your pooch become bored with the same old game of fetch. This book contains fun, exciting activities to spark your interest plus get your dog's tail wagging again.

Dogs are some of the best playmates around. They're full of energy. They're always ready to play and eager to invent new games. They're loyal and devoted. Best of all, dogs offer unconditional love. It doesn't matter if you won the lead in the school play or fumbled the ball in the big game, if you aced the math test or burnt the brownies. Your dog will always adore you no matter what.

Your dog is a magnificent magician. He's able to snuggle his way into your heart. He can persuade you to explore the world at nose level. With the wag of a tail, your dog promises you a lifelong adventure. Now you can repay your furry friend.

This book is designed not just for reading, but for using every day. I hope sharing the activities in this book with your dog inspires you along the way to a rewarding relationship. The more time you spend together, the more fun you'll both have!

Before you begin the fun stuff, you should make sure your dog is in great shape. Schedule an appointment for your vet to examine your pet. He'll help your pet to live a longer and healthier life. And don't forget to give your dog a daily dose of love!

Understanding Your Dog

Did you know that dogs have lived with humans for at least 14,000 years? They were the first animals that we domesticated. Dogs similar to our modern breeds were painted on cave walls around the world.

Cavemen tamed wolf puppies as pets. Your dog is a descendant of the wolf. Just like wolves, your dog lives in a pack—it's just that for your dog, your family becomes her pack instead of other dogs. A tame dog is happiest when her human companion is the pack leader. She needs someone to love and respect.

Although dogs have been our companions for thousands of years, they still share many traits with wolves. Both show their moods through body language. You can learn how to "speak dog" by observing your pooch. A playful dog might bow down on her front legs, with her rear in the air and her tail wagging. An angry dog will bare her teeth, lay her ears back, and walk stiff-legged with a raised tail. A fearful dog will roll onto her back, tail tucked, and avoid eye contact. The affectionate dog will greet you with lots of face licking.

Wolves and dogs communicate through barking, howling, growling, whimpering, and through body language. They greet each other by sniffing the tail and muzzle areas. Both wolves and dogs have super senses compared to humans. Your dog can hear high sounds that cannot be heard by you. Your dog can smell odors so faint your nose would never detect them. And while your dog cannot see colors as well as you, she does see more clearly in dim light than you.

As cavemen's pet wolves became tamer, the cavemen found out that they could breed dogs to bring out different features. They discovered that if you bred two smaller dogs, you typically got a small dog. Likewise, if you bred two friendly dogs, you usually got a friendly one. Gradually, these original wolf pets became man's—and woman's—best friend: the domestic dog.

Today there are almost 400 different breeds of dogs worldwide. Each has special characteristics. Dogs have been bred for many uses such as herding sheep, pulling sleds, and snuggling on laps.

Dogs are available in many shapes, sizes, and colors. Despite their different outward appearances, they are all the same species—*canis familiaris*.

Our country is literally going to the dogs. An estimated 36 million homes in America contain at least one dog. That's quite a menagerie!

Picking the Perfect Pooch

If you don't have one already, how can you pick the perfect pooch? First, you need to decide whether your new companion should be male or female. Either can make an outstanding pet. Males grow larger than females. While males can be more energetic and playful, they also might be more aggressive and territorial. Females can be less dominant and easier to train, but they also might need more affection and interaction.

Next, you should think about whether a puppy or grown dog will fit in best with your family. Puppies demand constant attention, housebreaking, and someone who can patiently spend large amounts of time with them. Adult dogs don't require such a huge chunk of time. An adult dog's personality can be easily observed, while it may be hard to tell what a puppy will turn out to be like. As a bonus, adult dogs are usually house-trained and might be familiar with obedience commands. A grown dog is a much better choice if someone isn't home most of the day.

Which breed of dog is right for you? Before you adopt, you need to do some research to assure a perfect match. Make a list of features you want your new canine companion to have. Should she be large and full of energy for hikes in the mountains? Or should she be shorthaired and streamlined for catching a Frisbee?

If you're not sure just what kind of dog is right for you, there are a couple of Web sites that can help you pick a breed. The tests are free and a lot of fun to take.

Go to http://www.purina.com/dogs/index.html and follow the link to their "breed selector." Their Q & A will help guide you in choosing a dog. Take the test a couple of times to get an idea of what breed is right for you. Purina's Web site also has some great information on feeding and care.

Another good site to help you choose a dog is Glowdog's Web site at http://www.glowdog.com. Once there, follow the link to "Which breed is best for you?" You'll answer a questionnaire and they'll provide you with a list of good candidates based on the importance level of each question. Once you do decide on a dog, Glowdog offers some reflective clothing items for you and your dog to protect you at night.

Read books about individual breeds in which you are interested. These will describe canine characteristics. Discover what the pros and cons are in the breeds that have grabbed your attention. You can never know too much about a breed. The more you understand, the easier it will be to make a smart decision. Keep in mind that each dog is unique. No two are alike in personality.

You can zero in on different breeds anywhere dogs gather: the veterinary clinic, obedience classes, kennels, groomers, breeders, breed rescue groups, animal shelters, and humane societies. Visit dog shows and events to see a great variety of breeds and ask the handlers questions.

When you go, always remember to *ask* permission before petting an unfamiliar dog. Not only is it more polite to ask permission but some dogs are very territorial and protective and may snap at you.

There is also a proper and a wrong way to pet a dog. Don't come right up to the dog and bring your hand down fast onto her head. A dog will take that as a threatening gesture. First you should kneel down so you are at the dog's level. With your fingers curled into a loose fist, bring your hand slowly to just beneath the dog's nose. Let her sniff your closed hand. Once she relaxes, you can pet her chest and under her chin.

Here's a "Who's Zoo" of dogs, which the American Kennel Club has divided into seven groups.

Sporting breeds were originally bred as gun dogs to locate and retrieve game. They include the pointers, setters, spaniels, and retrievers. These dogs enjoy plenty of outdoor exercise, such as swimming and hiking. Sporting breeds love to interact with people. The popular Labrador and Golden Retrievers are intelligent, dependable, and alert, and are often used as guide dogs for the blind.

Hounds, the oldest breed, are divided into two groups. Scenthounds, such as the Beagle and Bloodhound, have a keen sense of smell and more stamina than speed. Sighthounds, such as the Greyhound and Whippet, rely on sight rather than scent and are speedy. These dogs love to chase other animals.

Working breeds were bred for a variety of jobs. Alaskan Malamutes pull sleighs and Newfoundlands haul carts. Akitas and Doberman Pinschers are guardians and watchdogs. Most are large energetic dogs. Working dogs excel at search-and-rescue and assisting the police.

Terriers, or earth dogs (from the Latin word, *terra*, meaning earth or ground) were originally used to dig for and drive out small game. These lively and aggressive dogs include the Wire-haired Fox Terrier and the Staffordshire Bull Terrier. Terriers are courageous and playful, and share a love of digging.

Toy breeds are household pets bred for companionship. Many, such as the Pekinese, are from the Orient and were brought back by explorers as gifts. Several, like the Miniature Pinscher, were bred down in size from larger dogs. Most toys weigh less than ten pounds. Despite their size, they are assertive and demand to be spoiled.

Non-sporting breeds were bred for a purpose for which they are no longer used. Bulldogs were originally used for bullbaiting, Dalmatians for running alongside coaches, and Poodles as water retrievers. Today, their primary purpose is companionship.

Herding breeds guard and control livestock. Since their herding instinct is strong, they sometimes round up children, too. Collies herd with their bodies; Welsh Corgies drive livestock by barking and nipping at the heels. These intelligent dogs are active and need exercise to keep from becoming bored.

If you are searching for a special dog that combines the best features of many breeds, consider the mutt, also known as the mongrel or mixed breed. This one-of-a-kind dog is the most common canine in the world.

There is nothing ordinary, however, about mutts. They come in all combinations, sometimes of surprising variety. It's as if Mother Nature decided to create designer dogs by mixing and matching.

Those that belong to the great mutt family usually display intelligence and a happy-go-lucky nature. These marvelous mixes might be without pedigrees, but they more than make up for it in personality!

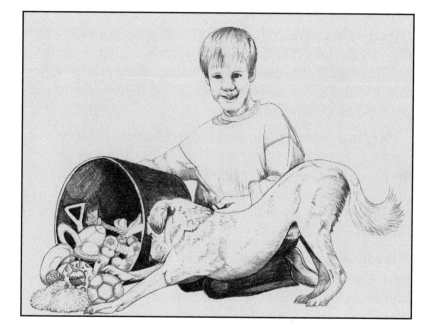

Pethouse

New puppy or older dog, each of them needs stuff to set-
tle into your household.

All dogs need a clean and comfortable place to sleep.
This can range from a trimmed-down cardboard box lined
with towels to a four-poster bed with silk cushions.
Whichever you choose, the bed's location is of top importance. Select a peaceful corner away from the hubbub. A
sleeping dog should never be disturbed.

Here's a hint to make a new puppy feel right at home.
Ask the breeder to put a small towel in with the litter the
day before you pick him up. When you take the puppy
home, lay this towel across his bed. Then he will still be
able to smell his mother and littermates.

Puppies love to explore. They're bursting with curiosity,
so you'll have to puppy-proof your home. Lie on the floor
to get a dog's eye view of potential trouble. Remove any-
thing that could cause problems if chewed. Enclose elec-
trical wires in plastic tubing. Secure screens on windows
and doors, and lids on garbage cans. You can put up a
baby gate to limit your puppy's access to one room.

Find another quiet spot for your pooch's bowls. These
should be made out of stainless steel and washed out
every day. Always have a bowl full of clean, cool water
available.

Chow time should be at the same time each day. Feed a
high-quality nutritious food that contains a good source
of protein, such as chicken. Ask your vet's advice about
what is right for your pet and be sure to ask if there are
any common food allergies particular to your breed of
dog. Then read the label for a guide on how much and

how many times a day to feed. This is usually based on your dog's age and weight.

Treats can be homemade goodies or store-bought biscuits. Keep in mind that they'll add calories to your pet's diet, so easy does it. Snacks shouldn't amount to more than ten percent of your dog's diet. After all, you don't want him to resemble the Goodyear blimp! Some dogs enjoy healthy human treats such as string cheese, carrots, green beans, frozen grapes, apples, and popcorn minus the butter and salt. Check with your vet if your pooch becomes paunchy.

Dogs love to chew almost as much as they enjoy eating. They can be piranhas when they're teething—which lasts until the ages of four to six months for most breeds. You can soothe a teething puppy by giving him a frozen treat. First, wet a clean washcloth. Wring it out. Then put the washcloth in the freezer until it's frozen solid. The iciness numbs teething pain.

If your puppy accidentally nips, you should yip in a high-pitched squealing voice. That's the sound his littermates would make if they were nipped. This will let him know he hurt you. Give him something to chew on without delay.

Avoiding Boredom

Get your pooch off on the right paw by giving him a variety of chew toys. You might be tempted to share toys with your best pal. Don't! Choose toys designed especially for dogs, otherwise socks, shoes, and human toys will all end up becoming dog toys. Toys designed especially for dogs can stand up to hours of doggy chewing. Be sure to replace all worn toys before pieces can be bitten off and swallowed.

Here are some ideas to toy around with. Try wolf-sized rawhide and synthetic bones. Maybe your pet would prefer a squeaky porcupine that massages his gums. A hard nylon ring can be rolled around in circles. Or try stuffing a bouncing rubber toy with a mixture of biscuit, carrot, and peanut butter to keep him busy for hours. A fleecy stuffed bunny is great for your pal to snuggle up with— many pet toy manufacturers make fleecy toys designed especially for dogs that are sturdy and comforting as they will hold your scent. Soon you'll need a toy chest to hold everything!

To keep your pooch from becoming bored, try rotating the toys. You can offer a different toy each day of the week.

Outfit your dog with a nylon or leather leash and collar. For the correct collar size, measure around your pet's neck and add two to three inches to the measurement. Check the fit often as he grows. You should be able to slip two fingers between your dog's neck and the collar.

Attach a current license and ID tag with your name and your pet's name, address, and phone number—it could be your dog's ticket home if he becomes lost. At night, clip on a flashing red light like the kind joggers wear.

Then, take him for a walk. Daily exercise keeps dogs happy and healthy. An exercised dog doesn't need to release pent-up energy by chewing, digging, and barking. And walking socializes your pet by introducing him to new people, places, and animals. Bring along your poop-er-scooper or plastic baggies that you can turn inside out to pick things up with, seal, and then throw out in a trash can.

First Aid

Why not put together a K-911 first aid kit for your best friend? If an accident happens, you'll help your pet feel better on the way to the vet's office. Use a fishing tackle box or plastic container to store the items. Inside the top, tape your vet's phone number along with the twenty-four-hour emergency clinic phone number. Keep the kit in a pet-safe location.

Here are some of the things you'll need: safety scissors, cotton swabs and balls, gauze pads and bandages, adhesive tape, hydrogen peroxide, styptic powder, tweezers, muzzle, wound powder or ointment, and antihistamine for insect bites. Include an extra leash and collar with tags, a copy of your pet's medical records, and recent color photos of your pet in case he gets lost and you need to make a poster.

The Vet

Besides you, your dog's next best friend is the veterinarian. Ask other dog lovers to recommend a good vet. Then visit with your dog. The clinic should look and smell clean. The vet you select should be easy to communicate with and answer any questions you ask.

Your puppy's first appointment should be scheduled when he is eight weeks of age, or soon after you adopt him if he is older than eight weeks. The vet will start a series of vaccinations. Until they are complete, you will need to keep your puppy safely away from other pets and people.

The annual physical exam, where your dog gets examined, weighed, and receives yearly vaccines and heartworm and parasite testing, will go smoother if you practice at home. Teach your dog to stand still as you check his ears and eyes, open his mouth, pick up his feet, inspect under his tail, and run your hands along his back, chest, and belly. If you do this regularly, you can also spot problems earlier.

Healthy Hounds

Another way to catch health problems is to recognize what's normal for your dog. Know the signs of a healthy pet. The hair and skin should be clean, with no dandruff, fleas, or doggy odor. The eyes should be clear and bright, with no discharge. Ears should not be waxy or oily, and should be odor free. The nose should be moist and not running. Gums should be pink and firm, teeth gleaming white, and his breath should be fresh. The area under the tail should be clean.

Your dog should be neither too fat nor too thin. You should be able to feel his ribs when running your fingers along the dog's sides. Healthy dogs have high-energy levels and good appetites. They are lively and friendly, with a vibrant personality.

One of the greatest ways to show your dog you care is to spay her or neuter him. This safe surgery should be done as soon as possible, usually when your pet is around six months old. It will make your dog happier and healthier.

Neutered males are less likely to roam and fight with other dogs as they search for a mate. And spayed females will not have puppies that add to the pet overpopulation problem.

Did you know that in six years, one female dog and her offspring could give birth to 67,000 puppies? Each year, millions of wonderful dogs are put to sleep because there are not enough adoptive homes. Having your dog spayed or neutered is the responsible thing to do.

Pawsitive Obedience 101

Show your dog you love her by training her. Teach your pet good manners and you'll always have a wonderful companion.

Dogs learn quickly when you are positive. Never hit or yell at your dog. She needs to know that you'll never get angry with her, especially when she makes a mistake. You want your dog to trust you and feel safe. She's looking to you for guidance. Be kind, but firm.

Start to train your dog from the very first day. You will need a collar with an ID tag and a six-foot leash. Exercise your dog first so she'll be calm and relaxed, then find a quiet area, inside or outdoors, to teach her these basic obedience commands.

Training Fundamentals

When training, be sure to praise your dog each time she does something right. Speak in your happiest voice. Always use your dog's name: "What a good dog, Diamond." Smile and clap your hands. Make a big fuss over her. Give her a big hug and tell her she's the greatest. Believe me, it's impossible to give your dog too much attention!

In the beginning, you may need to offer her rewards, such as bits of cheese or slices of hot dog. Quick games with her favorite toy or a play session are additional rewards. Later, your praise and affection will be enough.

If you see your dog misbehaving, say "no" in a loud, sharp voice. You can also use something noisy to stop her from misbehaving. Place a few pennies in an empty soda can, then seal the opening with duct tape. It makes a terrific rattle when shaken. Remember, you *must* catch your pet in the act. Dogs have short memories. They will not know what they are being punished for if you wait even a few minutes.

Keep these obedience lessons short. Training time should last about five minutes for a puppy and twenty minutes for an adult dog. Dogs learn best by repetition.

Plan at least one session in the morning and one in the evening. This way neither of you will run out of patience. End each obedience session on a positive note. Your dog will always be eager for her next lesson.

Don't confuse your dog. Teach one command at a time. Your dog's name should go before each command. That way you can be sure she'll pay attention. Say each command only once, clearly and loudly. Everyone in your family should use the same command. When your dog has completed the exercise, release her with the word "okay." As she masters each command, her confidence will grow.

Basic Obedience

Here are some basic commands to turn your pooch into "Citizen Canine."

Sit Stand in front of your dog. Hold a treat or a toy in front of her nose. Raise the treat or toy above your dog's nose and forehead. Give the sit command. "Diamond, sit." As your dog looks up at the reward, her rear will begin to lower. Praise the dog when she is fully seated. Give her the treat or toy immediately.

If your dog looks up at the reward, but does not sit, use your other hand to press her rump down gently. Hold your pet in place as you praise her and give her the reward.

Down First, sit your dog. Squat down beside her. Lower a treat or toy to the ground in front of the dog's feet. Give the down command. "Diamond, down." She will follow the treat or toy downward, lowering the front portion of her body. Praise her when she is flat on the ground. Give her the treat or toy immediately.

If your dog looks down at the reward, but does not lie down, lift one front leg and lightly push on the opposite shoulder. Hold your pet in place as you praise her and give her the reward.

Stay Sit your dog. Stand beside her. Using a sweeping motion, bring your open palm in front of your dog's face. Give the stay command: "Diamond, stay." Then step out in front of the dog and face her. Next, take a few steps backward. Hold the stay for a few seconds. If your dog remains in place, go back to her side. Praise your pet.

If your dog gets up and follows you, say, "No," and begin again. Bring the dog back to the spot where you told her to stay. Take it slowly. Step in front of the dog, but do not take any steps back. Praise her when she stays and then release her with an "Okay!"

Start adding a few more seconds of time to this exercise each day. When your dog can stay in place for three minutes, take an extra step backward. In time your dog will master longer sit/stays at farther distances. Then you can practice the stay exercise with her lying down.

Come Use a six-foot-long leash. Sit your dog and command her to stay. "Diamond, stay." Walk to the end of the leash. Crouch down and look at your dog. Give the come command. "Diamond, come." Reel your dog in like a fish. When she reaches you, give her a hug and plenty of praise. Soon you will be able to practice this exercise off the leash.

Be sure you never use the come command to call your dog to you for a scolding. She will connect the command with punishment.

Heel Begin with your dog sitting at your left side. Take the leash in your right hand. Give the heel command. "Diamond, heel." Walk, starting off with your left foot. Your dog's right shoulder should be in line with your left hip.

If you walk along a fence or wall on your left, this exercise will be easier. Encourage your dog by talking as you walk. You can also hold a treat in your left hand so your dog lines up with you. She should not pull at the leash.

If your dog lags behind or forges ahead, use a quick, sharp tug on the leash. Immediately loosen the leash again. Once she is in the proper position, praise her as you continue walking.

Begin by walking short distances in a straight line. When you stop, give your dog the sit command.

Once your pet has mastered heeling, you can practice changes in pace and direction. You can vary your speed from normal to slow or fast. Circling to the right and to the left and making figure eights could also be worked into the heeling routine.

Off From the beginning, you should teach your pup not to jump on you or other people. Do not pet your dog if she does. You'll be rewarding bad behavior.

When your dog jumps up on you, lean forward and gently nudge her off with your knee. Give the off command: "Diamond, off." Then tell her to sit. "Diamond, sit." Show your approval by praising.

Drop It This comes in handy when you're playing fetch. Wait until your dog is carrying an object. Tell her to drop it. "Diamond, drop it." Never pull the object out of her mouth. Wait until she lets go of it herself. Then praise her when she drops it.

Hurry Up You'll use this command to help speed up housebreaking. Keep your puppy on a consistent schedule. Here's a typical plan: first thing in the morning (the instant your puppy wakes up), fifteen minutes after eating and drinking, after naps, after playtime, before bedtime. Be sure to remove the water bowl after dinner until she's housebroken.

Bring your puppy outside on a leash immediately. Choose an area for her to go to the bathroom. Always return to the same spot. Keep her moving. Give the command for your puppy to go to the bathroom: "Diamond, hurry up." When she goes, give her praise and a tiny treat.

Remember that puppies are babies. They don't have control of their muscles until they're about four months old. Accidents are certain to happen. When they do, don't hit your pup or rub her nose in the mess. She wouldn't understand why she's being punished, and will only end up being afraid of you.

You know she's sniffing out a spot to go to the bathroom when you see the puppy walking in circles. If you catch her performing the act, say "no" in a deep, low voice, or shake your soda can rattle. Quick, both of you make a beeline to her bathroom spot and then praise her when she goes.

Clean all mistakes right away. Then use a stain and odor neutralizer to remove the scent so she won't go there again. Take her, along with one of the soiled paper towels, outside. Place the paper towel in the spot she's chosen for her bathroom. Housebreaking will go smoothly if you help prevent accidents by sticking to your schedule like clockwork.

Making it More Fun

A fun way to rehearse some basic commands is with a round robin.

Ask several friends to stand in a circle around your dog. One at a time, let each person call your dog. "Diamond, come." Have that person offer your pet a treat, then give the command to sit. "Diamond, sit." Once your dog is sitting, release her to the next person by saying, "Okay, Diamond." Go around the circle until everyone has had a turn.

Advanced Obedience

Another terrific method for your dog to learn is for the two of you to join an obedience class. Just as in school, there are many different grade levels, from puppy kindergarten through advanced. Each dog learns at a different speed. Most can be trained to be obedient.

Professional training can help encourage good behavior. The trainer can also help with any problems you are having. As a bonus, your dog will rub shoulders with other canines in the class.

Before signing up, inquire about the training techniques used in class. You want to look for humane training, with no harsh punishments. Ask the trainer if you can watch a class in action.

After each obedience class, do your homework with your pooch by practicing the exercises every day. Along with teaching your dog, you'll be learning yourself!

Once your dog has mastered basic training skills, she can take the American Kennel Club's Canine Good Citizen Test. This series of ten steps demonstrates your dog's good manners. Your canine companion will show off her stuff by sitting politely for petting and walking through a crowd.

Many local groups and organizations offer this program. And any dog can earn a certificate. Frame it to let everyone know your dog is a well-behaved, valued member of the community. Congratulations! You should be very proud of your obedient dog.

*The great pleasure of a dog is that you may
make a fool of yourself with him and not only
will he not scold you, but he will make
a fool of himself, too.*
—Samuel Butler

*It is fatal to let any dog know that he is funny,
for he immediately loses his head
and starts hamming it up.*
-P. G. Wodehouse

Dogs laugh, but they laugh with their tails.
-Max Eastman

FUN FACT: Puppies don't wag their tails until
about thirty days after birth.

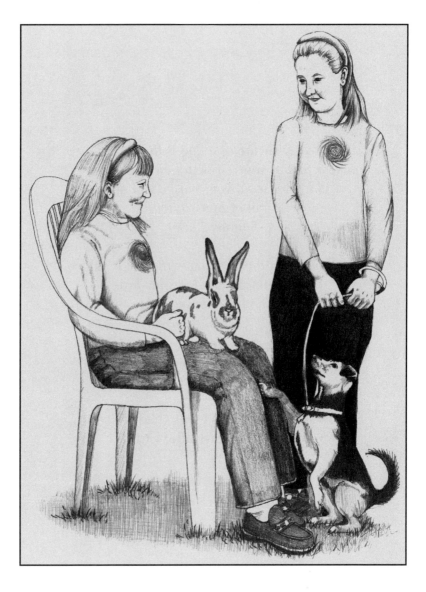

Bonding with Bowser

There is a strong bond between people and their dogs. Some even believe that their pets are mind readers. Is this a tall "tail"? Or could your dog have ESP? Here's one way to find out.

Choose a time when your pet is relaxed. Say your dog's name. Picture yourself and your dog going for a walk. Imagine the sights, sounds, and smells. If your dog acts as if you just suggested taking a walk then maybe he should get his own psychic phone line.

Pets are like furry Sherlock Hounds. They can detect your moods. Perhaps they're observing body language— your facial expressions, body position, and how you move. After all, this is how dogs communicate among themselves.

Your tone of voice is another clue. If you have a happy tone, your dog will also be cheerful. If you're sad, your best pal will be down in the dumps. So keep a smile on your face!

Mutt Monikers

Dogs quickly learn to respond to their names. Sometimes Rover, Fido, or Spot just wouldn't do. So how do you pick the perfect name for your canine companion?

Perhaps the best way to select a name is to spend time observing your pet. Don't rush. Try several names. Which one does he answer to? If you're lucky, maybe your dog will help you pick his own name.

Does your new pooch have a distinguishing feature? A puppy with melting chocolate eyes could be named after your favorite chocolate bar. Maybe your dog sounds like a bongo when he taps out a rhythm with his tail. My own dog, Diamond Dreamer, who is a black lab mix, has a distinctive white diamond on her chest and animated dreams.

What funny antic does your dog perform? Perhaps he spins around like a tornado or twists into funny shapes resembling a pretzel. Is he the spitting image of a famous person or another creature? A dog that likes to explore might answer to Columbus; while a mammoth mongrel could be called T-Rex.

The month in which your dog was born or the country where his ancestors came from might provide ideas. Always choose a name that will grow with your dog (it may not be best to name a Great Dane "Tiny"). Get other family members to join in the name game—it could continue for days!

Your dog will quickly learn his own name. At the sound of it, he'll turn his head toward you. Always include him in all your conversations. Soon you'll be carrying on a dogalogue with your pet—just like Dr. Doolittle!

Four Paws Up

Here's a fun way to let your dog know how much you treasure those special moments together. On a rainy day, snuggle close with your pooch and watch a video movie starring your favorite canine characters. Here are some that get four paws up from Diamond:

- *The Adventures of Milo and Otis* (1989) — When his feline friend is swept down a river, Otis the Pug is off to the rescue.
- *Air Bud* (1997) — A Golden Retriever with a talent for playing basketball befriends a boy who needs a buddy.
- *All Dogs Go to Heaven* (1989) — A gangster dog

returns from Heaven to earth, where a little girl teaches him a lesson in love.

- *Babe* (1995) — After being fostered by a Border Collie, an orphaned talking piglet believes he's a Sheepdog.
- *Beethoven* (1992) — A Saint Bernard who adopts a family must escape the clutches of a villainous veterinarian.
- *Benji* (1974) — The shaggy mutt falls in love and foils an attempt to kidnap two children.
- *A Dog of Flanders* (1959) — A brutally beaten dog is restored to health by a young Dutch boy and his grandfather.
- *Far from Home: The Adventures of Yellow Dog* (1995) — After their boat capsizes, a teen and his faithful yellow Labrador Retriever struggle for survival in the British Columbia wilderness.
- *The Incredible Journey* (1963) — Homeward bound, a Labrador Retriever, Bull Terrier, and Siamese cat take an adventurous trek across Canada.
- *Lad: A Dog* (1961) — A prize-winning Collie's love inspires a young girl to walk again.
- *Lady and the Tramp* (1955) — This animated classic features a spoiled Cocker Spaniel and a carefree mixed breed who fall in love.
- *Lassie, Come Home* (1943) — A thousand miles can't separate the famous Collie from his beloved boy.
- *Old Yeller* (1957) — A stray yellow hunting dog saves a pioneer teen's life, but tragically contracts rabies in the process.
- *101 Dalmatians* (1961) — When Pongo and Perdita's pups are kidnapped, they race to the rescue in this animated film starring a total of 6,469,952 spots.
- *Return of Rin Tin Tin* (1947) — This courageous German Shepherd, who was the first canine star,

rescues a refugee boy.

- *The Shaggy Dog* (1959) — After a boy is transformed into a spy-catching shaggy dog, he causes havoc for all those around him.
- *Shiloh* (1996) — A boy rescues and cares for a mistreated hunting Beagle belonging to a nasty hermit.
- *Where the Red Fern Grows* (1974) — A pair of inseparable Red-Bone Hounds guide a boy on his voyage to maturity in Dust-Bowl era Oklahoma.
- *Zeus and Roxanne* (1997) — A Portuguese Podengo dog strikes up an amazing friendship with a dolphin.

Bring on the pup-corn!

Mutt Massages

Another great way to share quality time with your dog is to give him a massage. Most dogs relish a relaxing rubdown. Older canines with arthritis will especially appreciate it. Massage soothes your dog's aching muscles. Plus, it strengthens the trust between you and your pet.

Wait until your pet is in a calm mood. Let him stretch out on his side. This is a naturally relaxing position. A towel or rug underneath will make him more comfortable. Use your thumbs to draw tiny clockwise circles. Take your time: slower is better. Start massaging up and down on either side of the spine. Use a medium pressure going up and a light pressure going back down. Slowly work your way across your pet's entire back.

If your dog enjoys having a back massage, you might continue with other parts of the body, such as the forehead, back of neck, and legs. Massaging the center tips of the ears calms restless dogs. Soon your pet will be begging for these relaxing sessions!

Did you know that the link between you and your dog

could be good for your own health? A furry companion can make you laugh, help you relax, and encourage you to exercise. Petting and stroking a dog can even lower your blood pressure. And caring for a pet helps people live longer.

Making Friends

Dogs are welcome visitors in many hospitals and nursing homes. These therapy dogs make wonderful cheerleaders. They can calm patients and make them smile. Once your pet has mastered the basic commands, check whether pet visitation programs exist near you.

Fido can also bond with four-legged friends. Other dogs, cats, rabbits, and additional pets can become lifelong buddies, depending on your dog's personality. Watching different species play and communicate with each other is fascinating and rewarding.

It's best to introduce your dog to a new companion after he has completed obedience training. Start with another dog that is calm and mature. Keep your own dog on a leash at first. Supervise all encounters, which should start off being brief. Let them sniff each other and get acquainted. These on-leash sessions could range from several days to a few weeks, depending upon compatibility.

Offer your dog a lavish amount of praise and encouragement to keep him from becoming jealous of the newcomer: "What a good, gentle dog you are, Zeus." If your dog becomes too excited, tell him "off" or "no." Have him sit and stay as you remind him to be gentle. You are trying to set this relationship up to succeed and allowing your dog to become out of control will only set you up for failure. With practice and patience, soon they'll form a peaceable kingdom!

Pet Pics

Why not snap some photos of your dog for your wallet? This way your pal will always be close to you. The trick is to capture your dog's personality. You'll need lots of patience and several rolls of film.

Choose an uncluttered background. You might want to use your pet's favorite toy as a prop. By kneeling down, you can snap pictures at your pet's level. Have someone stand behind you with a squeaky toy to attract your furry model's attention. Take a variety of shots from different angles, including close-ups.

You can turn the best photo into a **Pet Portrait Magnet** for your locker. Here's how.

Pet Portrait Magnet

Materials:

Photo of your pet
Plastic jar lid (lightweight, like the top from a can of Pringles)
Pencil
Scissors
Glue (a strong glue, like an epoxy)
Small magnet
Cotton swab

1. Place your photo face up on a flat surface. Then cover the portion of the photo you want to use with the lid. You can use a close-up head shot or a small picture of your pet.

2. With the pencil, carefully trace around the lid. Use the scissors to cut out the photo around the circle you drew.

3. Cover the top of the lid with glue. Now place your photo on top of the glue so it covers the entire lid. Use your fingers to smooth and press down the photo. Allow to dry for one hour.

4. Now turn the lid over. Put a dab of glue inside the lid. Center your magnet in the glue. Press firmly down on the magnet with a cotton swab.

5. Remove the swab and allow the glue to dry thoroughly.

Now you can decorate your locker with your Pet Portrait Magnet.

Games Dogs Play

Does your dog yawn and go back to sleep when you try to get her interested in a game of fetch? Well, put away the balls and sticks and try these new games. Her tail will soon be wagging again.

Doggy Obstacle Course

You can set up this course in a large room or a securely fenced backyard. Use a combination of old tires and cardboard boxes to make a tunnel your dog can crawl through. A piece of PVC tubing balanced on two boxes or chairs makes a nifty low jump. Scrunch up three towels and lay them in a row to create a broad jump. A narrow plank or log can be transformed into a balance beam. Push together picnic benches or boxes to make a maze that your dog can walk through. Use your imagination for even more obstacles.

You can team up and race through the obstacle course together. For double the fun, invite another dog to join in. Play keeps a dog's body and mind active!

Spot's Sports

Your pooch is ready and raring to go. It's almost as if she wakes up each morning yelling, "Yahoo!" Lots of exercise will help your dog burn off extra energy. Make it a daily routine. Start the fitness program off slowly. Begin with a warm-up and finish with a cool-down. And if your dog has just dined, wait for at least an hour before exercising.

Match the breed with the activity. For dogs who like to chase, capture, and retrieve, hit tennis balls or bat wiffle balls. Dogs bred for herding could join you in flying a kite.

Diggers, such as terriers, might relish digging in a sand-box where you've buried a special treasure for them to discover. Scenthounds especially love to use their noses to track hidden treats. A dog that enjoys running could join alongside as you jog or rollerblade. Swimmers will be eager to combine a dip with retrieving sticks and floating toys.

Sniff and Seek

There's no doubt about it—all dogs love to play this game! Take your dog's favorite toy and put a dab of peanut butter on it. Then let her sniff the toy. Have her sit and stay. Hide the toy in an obvious place, such as under a towel a few feet away. Next, encourage your doggy detective to "find it." Make a big fuss when she does.

Soon you can hide the toy a little farther away, where it is more difficult to find. Just make sure your dog will be able to reach it. Sit your dog with her back towards you. No fair peeking! Now tell your dog to "find it." Don't help her or she'll learn to expect it. Your dog needs a fun activity to do all by herself.

You could even try hiding yourself! You'll both have hours of fun on the rainiest day.

Canine Contests

You will need two or more dogs and plenty of treats. Every dog should be awarded a doggy biscuit for participating.

- Tie one end of a rope to a stick and tie the other end to a biscuit. Dangle the biscuit and see which dog jumps highest.
- Let the dogs bob for dog biscuits. This will get messy, so break out the bibs or do the activity outdoors. Fill up a dishpan with water. Drop in a

handful of dog biscuits. Wait until they sink to the bottom of the dishpan. Cheer on the dogs as they dunk and drool. Who has the biggest haul?

- Pop a big batch of popcorn. Place the dogs in a row, sitting. Then throw kernels of popcorn in the air and watch who catches the most.
- Have a relay race. Pair up dogs with human partners. Who will cross the finish line first?
- How about a tail wagging contest? Which dog can wag the longest? Whose tail is the fastest? This will leave your head vibrating!
- Are you ready for a tough one? Line up the doggy contestants. On your mark, get set, go! Each person throws out a hot dog and yells "fetch." Encourage your dog to retrieve her hot dog and bring it back to you—uneaten! This contest is good for lots of laughs.

Frisbee and Flyball

These two events have become extremely popular competitive sports for dogs. Training your dog for either one can be an extra-special time. So shake out those paws and follow these beginner tips.

Frisbee

Frisbee events have grown into one of our great national pastimes for dogs. These canine competitions originated in 1974, when a four-legged athlete named Ashley Whippet thrilled the crowds at Dodger Stadium with his nine-foot leaps in the air to catch discs.

Today, dogs of every imaginable size and breed are joining in the high-flying dog Olympics. It's a fun, competitive experience. First, check with your vet to make sure your dog is in tip-top shape. Puppies should be at least fourteen months old before attempting to leap high for a Frisbee.

To play catch-and-retrieve Frisbee you'll need a team: one dog and one thrower. The object of the game is to make as many successful throws/catches as possible.

First, get your dog interested in the disc. Roll it along the ground, like a wheel. If this doesn't excite your dog, slide the disc on the ground in circles in front of him. You can even give your dog a drink out of the disc.

Another way to grab your dog's interest is to play keep-away with a friend. Roll or slide the disc back and forth between you and your friend. Let your dog intercept the disc as soon as he shows interest.

Now it's time to encourage your dog to fetch and retrieve the disc. Put your dog on a long leash. When he grabs the disc, tell him to come and reel him in. Give him tons of praise.

Once your dog reaches you, you'll need him to drop the disc. Give the "drop it" command and point to the ground. Offer your dog a toy or treat to encourage him—he'll eagerly drop the Frisbee for his favorite treat. Praise him again. Once he gets the idea, try it off-leash.

As soon as your dog learns this, he's ready for the next step—catching the disc in the air. Start off with low, flat throws. Make your dog run to catch the disc. Don't throw it in his direction.

Never throw the disc directly at the dog. If you hit him, he might become afraid of the flying disc. Take your time and have fun. Quit when your pooch loses interest.

This step could take some time to master. Be patient. Canine disc play is a team effort. Soon your dog will be soaring through the air, catching the Frisbee in mid-flight!

After your dog masters the basics, you might enjoy entering one of the community contests held throughout the country each year. In the mini-distance rounds, teams attempt to make as many successful throws/catches during two 60-second rounds. Points are awarded for catches beyond ten yards from the throwing line. Higher scores are given for mid-air catches.

Or you can compete against your friends and their dogs. Which dog can catch the most discs in one minute? Which can jump the highest? Which can catch the farthest long-distance throw? You might want to borrow a crank-type plastic measuring tape for this last one.

Always play Frisbee catch in a safe, grassy area. Avoid asphalt or concrete, which could injure you or your four-legged athlete. Bring along plenty of fresh water for the canine competitors. Finally, make sure you let your dog warm up slowly before a workout.

Flyball

Flyball is another team sport for dogs. It was also launched in the 1970s. In this heart-pounding game, the team consists of four dogs who run through a course relay-race style. Each dog crosses the starting line, jumps over four hurdles spaced ten feet apart, and bounces his paws against a spring-loaded Flyball box that shoots out a tennis ball. The canine contestant catches the tennis ball in his mouth, turns, and jumps back over the four hurdles. When the dog crosses the starting line, the next dog on the team goes.

These relay races last less than a minute, as each dog speeds down the 51-foot course. Two teams are pitted against each other—and the clock. Whichever team completes the course in the fastest time, without any mistakes such as dropping the ball, wins. Twenty seconds or less per dog is considered a good run.

Training for a Flyball tournament takes plenty of practice. Dogs don't master Flyball overnight. Most average six months to learn the routine. Break it down into steps. You can get your dog started off on the right paw with these tips.

The first step is to teach your dog to fetch a tennis ball. Only use balls with the felt covering, which are safe for dogs to catch and grip. Try throwing the ball into a corner so your dog must make a tight turn to come back to you. Also coach your dog by tossing the ball up a gently sloping incline.

Turn it into a game. Throw the ball and run away from the dog, telling him "come." This will encourage his chasing instinct and improve his speed. When he retrieves the ball, tell him "drop it" and blow gently in his nose until he does.

The next step is to train your dog to jump over four low hurdles in a straight line. In competition, eight inches is the minimum height. Start off with the hurdles at four inches high. Use pieces of plastic PVC tubing balanced on two boxes. Keep the hurdles close together so the dog takes a single bound between jumps. Later you can gradually move the hurdles until they are ten feet apart. Wave your dog's favorite toy over the hurdles to encourage him. Practice, and then slowly raise the height a half an inch at a time until it is eight inches.

In the last step your dog learns the "hit it" command. Instead of a Flyball box, you will use a square of carpet propped up with a sponge. Encourage your dog to touch the carpet square. As soon as he does, say "hit it" and throw a tennis ball for him to catch. Presto! Soon your dog will be pouncing on the carpet to get the ball.

Now you and your dog can attend a Flyball tournament. If you both catch "Flyball fever," you might ask to join a team or start your own.

FUN FACT: About one-third of U. S. households
have one or more dogs.

*A dog is the only thing on this earth that loves you
more than he loves himself.*
—Josh Billings

FUN FACT: The canine population of the world
is said to number up to 150 million

Tricks for Treats

Is your dog weary of the same old routine? She's shaken paws so many times, she thinks she's a politician. When you ask her to roll over, she rolls her eyes instead. Don't worry. Even an old dog can be taught the new exciting tricks in this chapter.

Dogs learn through repetition, so practice often for short times (ten to fifteen minutes). Choose a trick your dog might enjoy performing. It should be fun for both of you!

Some tricks might take longer to learn. Your pet won't become a magician of tricks overnight. No two dogs learn at the same rate. Don't worry —your dog will be exercising her brain as well as her body. Trick training helps dogs show off their intelligence. And it keeps them from getting bored and into mischief.

Remember, praise is what your dog lives for. Be generous with it!

Your family and friends will be amazed when your dog performs these tricks.

Tricks

Kiss This trick could not be simpler. Each time your dog licks you, say "kiss" and make a smooching sound. If she needs some encouraging, put a dab of peanut butter on your cheek. As your dog licks it off, say "kiss." Soon she'll connect the word with the action.

Wag Your Tail Here's another easy trick all dogs can perform. Using an excited voice, ask "Who's a happy dog?" Your dog will begin to wag her tail–or rear if she is tailless. Keep that tail moving by pouring on the praise.

Sing Begin with some high notes, either sing them or play them on a piano, harmonica, or recorder. Once your dog responds to this high-pitched sound, say "sing." She'll probably howl as long as the notes are being played. Wait until after she's done singing to make a big fuss over her.

Wave Bye-Bye Start with your dog in a sit/stay position. Sitting in front of your dog, wave your hand back and forth. Say "wave," and gently nudge your dog's front paw until she lifts it up. Use your hand to hold her paw chest-high for a second. Release her paw and reward her. Soon she'll respond to your hand signal alone.

Tag Hang a dog picture on the wall. Take your dog up to the picture and say "tag." Pat the picture with your hand. When your dog jumps up and touches the picture, reward her. Once your dog gets the idea, have her practice "tagging" different objects. Before long she'll join you in a game of tag with the neighborhood kids!

Car Wash Stand with your legs as far apart as your dog's body is wide. Use a treat to persuade your dog to go through your legs. As she does, rub your legs back and forth along the length of her body saying "car wash." After a few "test drives," your dog should zoom through your legs whenever you mention the words "car wash."

Rock 'n' Roll This one's great when you need your dog to shake off, such as after a bath or a walk in the rain. Bend over and gently blow in her ear, then say "rock 'n' roll." Your dog will shake from nose to tail.

Jump Through Hoops You'll need a friend to help with this circus trick. Have your friend hold a hula-hoop at ground level. Coax your dog to walk through the hoop, using a reward. Tell her "Jump!" When your dog masters going through the hoop each time you give her the command, have your helper raise the hoop off the floor. Go slowly, an inch at a time, encouraging your dog to jump. With practice, your dog will be leaping through the hoop like a circus star!

Dance Start with your dog in the sit position. Slowly lift a treat over her head until she is standing on her hind legs. Each day, increase the time by a few seconds. Some dogs keep their balance better than others.

When your dog easily stretches for the treat, it's time to teach a few dance steps. Select lively music for inspiration. Then urge your pet, "Dance like a circus dog." Move the treat in forward, backward, and sideways patterns above her head. She'll spin around if you circle the treat overhead. Don't keep your dog up for too long. Finish the dance recital with the next trick.

Take a Bow When your dog stretches—with her head down by the ground and her rear up in the air—it looks like she is bowing. Each time you see her stretch after a nap say "take a bow." Quick, give her a treat when she is in the bow position.

Crawl This trick is a combination of down and come. Tell your dog "down, stay." Place one hand over, but not touching, her back. With your other hand, hold a treat in front of her nose. Keep it close to the ground. Say "come" and start moving the treat away.

If she starts to get up, gently push her back down with your hand and command "down, come" again. You could also lure her under a low obstacle such as a picnic bench. If she moves even an inch or two, give her the treat. With enough practice, your dog will understand that she must crawl a little way before she gets rewarded.

Say Your Prayers Sit in a chair in front of your seated dog. Put a treat between your legs. Tell your dog "say your prayers" and lift both of her front paws onto the chair. The treat will be between her paws. She must remain seated. Your dog will stick her nose down between her paws to get the treat. As she does, say "amen" and then reward her with the treat. Soon she will be performing the trick on her own.

Card Sharpei   Your dog will use her nose to perform this trick. Hide a dab of peanut butter under your pinkie nail. Spread out a deck of cards. Ask someone to pick a card and hand it back to you. Shift the peanut butter from your nail onto the face of this card, where no one will see it.

Here is where you can exhibit your showmanship. Show the card to your dog. Tell her to concentrate as you tap your forehead with one finger.

Next, put the card face down on the bottom of the deck. Then turn the deck so the faces are toward you. Spread the cards out. Pick six cards from the deck, including the peanut butter card. Place these cards face down in a row on the floor. Leave some space between each card.

Tell your dog to find the chosen card. She will smell the peanut butter and pick the correct card.

FUN FACT: It is believed that the dog was the first animal to be domesticated.

If a dog's prayers were answered,
bones would rain from the sky.
–Old Proverb

FUN FACT: The Greyhound is the only breed of dog mentioned in the Bible (Proverbs 30:29-31), possibly because this sleek creature is one of the oldest of all breeds. But according to legend, the pair of dogs chosen by Noah to journey aboard his ark were Afghan Hounds.

Clever Canine Tests

Have you ever wondered just how smart your dog is? Now you can find out with this series of fun tests. Unlike the ones you take in school, these tests don't require your dog to study. All you need are a stopwatch and lots of praise. Are you ready? Let the fun begin.

Test 1 This will show how quickly your dog can solve a problem. Throw a towel over your dog's head. Start the stopwatch. Do not talk to your dog. See how long it takes him to remove the towel.

Score: Three points for freeing himself in 30 seconds or less. Two points for getting the towel off in 30 seconds to one minute. One point if the towel is still on his head after one minute.

Test 2 This will measure how observant your dog is. Grab your dog's attention. Then silently pick up his leash. Walk into the middle of the room.

Score: Three points if your dog runs to you or to the door. Two points if you have to walk to the door before your dog comes to you. One point if your dog ignores you.

Test 3 This is another problem-solving test. Show your dog a treat. Let your dog sniff the treat. Then put the treat under a plastic flowerpot. Start your stopwatch.

Score: Three points if your dog knocks over the pot and gets the treat in ten seconds or less. Two points for getting the treat in 11 to 60 seconds. One point if your dog does not try to get the treat.

Test 4 This test will determine your dog's comprehension skills. Have your dog sit across the room from you. Using your normal voice, call "Rumplestiltskin."

Score: Three points if your dog comes. If he does not come, call "rabbit." Score Two points if your dog comes this time. If he still does not come, call his name. Give him one point.

Add up the scores from the four tests. If the final score is 12, your dog is a genius. A score of 9-11 means your dog is very smart. If your dog scored 5-8 points, he is average. And the dog that scored 4 points is not the brightest, but you love him anyway. Give your dog extra attention. Then try the test again in two months. You might be surprised by the results!

A dog is like an eternal Peter Pan,
a child who never grows old and who therefore
is always available to love and be loved.
—Aaron Katcher

FUN FACT: Dogs have been featured in world
literature since the first century B.C., when
Roman writer Varro immortalized his sheepdog
in a book titled *Rerum rusticarum libri*.

Bow-Wow Birthday Fun

Your dog is a member of your family, so of course you'll want to celebrate her birthday in style. If you don't know the exact birth date, you can observe the anniversary of the day you brought your best pal home.

Begin with a guest list. Send out invitations two weeks ahead of the big date. You can make your own. Cut a large bone shape out of cardboard. Trace around it onto paper bags, then cut out the bones. List your dog's name, along with the date, time, and place of the party. Add your phone number so guests can RSVP. Instead of gifts, why not ask the partygoers to bring along some cans of dog food to donate to the local shelter?

When the hungry hounds arrive, serve them these **Planet K-9 Cookies** during Yappy Hour.

Planet K-9 Cookies

Ingredients:

One 6-ounce jar of baby food dinner
6 tablespoons wheat germ
4 tablespoons powdered milk
1 teaspoon of dried parsley

Diamond prefers vegetable chicken for the baby food, but you'll have to discover what your dog likes best. As long as it has meat in it of one kind or another, your dog should love it. Once you have all the ingredients, mix them all together in a medium-sized bowl. Form the mixture into eight ovals about the size of a tablespoon. Have an adult help you bake the cookies on a greased cookie sheet for 15 minutes in a 350° oven. Cool the cookies for

30 minutes. These go fast, so you might want to double or triple the recipe.

After the top dog has finished greeting her guests, have the partygoers gather for a group photo. They can wear matching party hats. Noisemakers are usually not necessary.

How about some party games? No dog can resist a hide-and-sniff treasure hunt. Before the four-footed guests arrive, you can hide rawhide chews around the room. Just make sure all the dogs can reach them. Turn the partygoers loose and let the fun begin!

Ready for another game? Here's a variation on musical chairs. Try some theme music, such as "How Much Is That Doggy in the Window?" and "Walking the Dog" and "Hound Dog." Put one person in charge of the music. When the song begins, have everyone walk their pets in a circle. When the person in charge of the music stops the song, everyone should halt and tell their dogs to sit. Last dog to sit is out. Repeat until there is one winner.

Your birthday pooch and her pals should have worked up an appetite by now. Gather the gang together for a rousing chorus of "Happy Bone-day." Then serve this **No-Bake Rover Cake** that they will all drool over.

No-Bake Rover Cake

Three 13-ounce cans of ground beef dog food
1 egg
1 cup bread crumbs

Mix all ingredients in a medium-sized bowl. If necessary, add more bread crumbs so the mixture will hold its shape. This is squishy, so you might want to don rubber gloves. Once it's mixed, dump the mixture onto a large platter covered with aluminum foil. Then mold it into a bone shape. Decorate around the sides with tiny puppy-sized dog biscuits.

You can also frost the top of the cake using low-fat cream cheese. If you want colored frosting, tint eight ounces of cream cheese with five drops of food coloring. Squeeze it through the small tip of a pastry tube to write your dog's name, initials, or draw her profile.

If you don't have a pastry tube, you can use a double sheet of heavy waxed paper rolled into a cone. Tape the edges, snip the tip for a small opening, twist the back end shut, and carefully squeeze the icing through, squeezing from the back. You might want to practice first on a slice of bread. Keep the cake refrigerated until the big event.

No doubt the partygoers would like to slurp some "dog-tails." The night before the party, freeze ice cube trays of chicken broth. Place a handful of these cubes in several dog bowls. Add water.

Don't send your pooch's canine pals home empty pawed. A few Planet K-9 Cookies wrapped up in the Bow-Wow Bandannas (on pages 69–70) make great doggy grab bags.

Can't you just see it? Your pooch's party is a howling success! The guests' tongues and tails are wagging for days. Already they are panting for next year's doggone invitation!

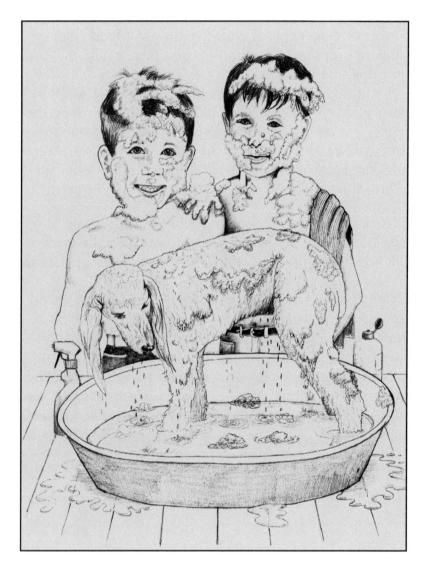

Mutt Makeovers

How would you feel if you only took a bath once a year? What if you never brushed your teeth or clipped your nails? Disgusting, right? Yet many dogs are only groomed annually.

Clean pets are healthier and happier. Here's how to transform that ball of fur into a grr-reat looking pet.

Grooming

Find a peaceful location. You can groom your pet on a table or while sitting alongside him on the floor. Turn on soft music–dogs prefer classical or jazz.

Brush your dog every day. This will keep his fur healthy and clean. As a bonus, brushing will pick up all the hair that your dog normally sheds. Most house dogs shed year round because they're exposed to artificial light and heat.

Start with the proper grooming tools. A wire slicker brush will remove tangles and loose hair on all types of fur. For short-haired dogs, add a hound glove. Long-haired dogs will need a pin brush and a wire comb with blunt teeth.

Beginning at the head, brush your dog's coat going in the direction his fur grows. Go slowly and gently. Talk as you brush. Tell him how gorgeous he will look. Continue until you reach the tip of the tail.

If you find a tangle, loosen it by lifting the hair and brushing it down, layer by layer. If it is still tangled, start at the end of the tangle (furthest from the skin) and gently run a wide-toothed comb through it. Slowly work your way up the tangle, a bit closer to the skin each time. Never yank your pet's hair. Grooming should be a pleasant experience, not scary or hurtful.

Next, rub your short-haired dog with the hound glove using downward strokes. Or comb through your long-haired dog's coat to make sure it is tangle-free.

Brushing is the first and most important step in dog grooming. It will release natural oils in his coat for a glossy sheen. If you brush your pet every day, he will need fewer baths. Bathe him only when he is dirty or if he has fleas.

Bath Time

Before the bath, the coat should be brushed free of tangles. Otherwise, mats will tighten the instant water hits them and they'll be impossible to remove.

You might ask an adult to help you with the bath. Your dog will shake, so it could be a good idea if you both wear waterproof grooming smocks. Use a rubber mat in the sink or tub so your dog doesn't slip.

Begin by plugging both of your dog's ears with cotton balls. Place a drop of mineral oil in each eye. Then, using a hand-held sprayer, wet your dog thoroughly with luke-warm water. Keep the water on the cool side. Your dog's skin is very sensitive.

Dilute some dog shampoo with water in an empty plastic squeeze bottle, like a dish washing detergent bottle. Begin at your dog's neck. Squeeze out some of the diluted shampoo in a circle all the way around his neck. This will keep any fleas from hiding on your pet's head or in his ears.

Now add more diluted shampoo and work your way down your dog's back, hindquarters, and belly. Save the face and ears for last.

Massage the shampoo into his fur. You can use your hands or a small rubber brush. Pay special attention to the ears, hindquarters, and feet.

Now you are ready to rinse out the shampoo. Again, use lukewarm water. When you get to the face, tip the dog's head up so no suds get into his eyes. Rinse thoroughly until the water runs clear.

With your dog in the tub, gently squeeze water from the fur with your hands. Towel as much water off the dog as possible. Keep your pet away from all drafts until dry. Or you can ask an adult to help you blow dry your pet. Use a forced air dryer on a cool setting and keep the dryer moving.

Fleas

During flea season, make a batch of **Disappearing Flea Juice**. Besides discouraging fleas, this all-natural remedy will give your pet's fur a super shine. Slice six lemons in half then put them into a one-quart glass jar. Ask an adult to pour boiling water over the lemons until the jar is full. Let the mixture stand for twenty-four hours.

Remove the lemons. Apply the liquid with a sponge as a dip or use a spray bottle and work into your dog's fur. Do not rinse.

To relieve the itching from those pesky bites, you can use aloe vera juice or gel. Purchase a bottle or make your own from an aloe vera plant. Snip off one of the leaves. Peel back the tough outer skin. The gel inside can be dabbed on bites to sooth and speed healing.

Pepé Lé Pew

Phew! Your pooch has tangled with a neighborhood skunk. If you don't remove the stinky scent, you'll smell skunk every time your dog gets wet. Bathe him immediately. Then apply a skunk odor remover. Skip the tomato juice–it will just tint your dog pink.

Ears

Once a week, check your dog's ears. Clean ears should be pink and odor free. If ears are not cleaned regularly they can become infected. Dogs with long, floppy ears have the most problems since air can't easily circulate.

Use cotton balls dipped in ear-cleaning solution to gently clean out excess wax. Careful–do not probe too far inside. Clean only the part of the inner ear that you can see.

Nails

The nails should be checked monthly. Too long nails can make it painful for your dog to walk. Have an adult help you with trimming them. Use special dog nail clippers to trim only the tips of the nails. If your dog becomes nervous, handle his paws and touch each nail often. Singing is a good way to distract and reassure him.

Avoid cutting the quick, or vein, which is easy to see in clear nails, but not black ones. If the nail is cut too close and it bleeds, apply a styptic made for pets. Don't forget to clip the dewclaws as well. You can use a dog nail file to smooth any rough edges.

Teeth

At least twice a week, brush your dog's teeth. If they are not cleaned, he will have bad breath, tartar, inflamed gums, and eventually lose teeth. Even worse, bacteria from infected gums could cause disease to his major organs.

Always use a toothbrush and toothpaste designed especially for dogs. Dogs can't spit out human toothpaste and it will irritate their tummies. Start off brushing just one tooth at a time. Slowly work your way up to cleaning all of the teeth. Brush both the teeth and gum line using a circular motion.

And your dog can floss his own teeth if you give him a cotton-fiber rope bone to chew on. The floss-like fibers will clean teeth and massage gums.

Keep that smile sparkling by selecting treats that will exercise teeth and massage gums: rawhides, nylon toys with raised dental nubs, hard biscuits, even carrots! Close encounters with your furry friend will be much sweeter.

Pampering Your Pooch

Sometimes your pooch just wants to be pampered. She will dazzle all of her friends when she wears this really cool doggy bandanna.

Bow-Wow Bandanna
Materials:

Sewing tape measure
Ruler
Pencil
Posterboard
Scissors
Chalk
Fabric

1. First, you'll need to take some simple measurements. Using a tape measure, find the distance around your dog's neck. Double this amount for the base of the triangular bandanna. Add six inches to your dog's neck size for the sides of the bandanna. For example, Diamond's neck measures 14 inches. The base of her bandanna is 28 inches; the sides are 20 inches.

2. Use a ruler and pencil to draw the triangle shape on a piece of posterboard. For a perfect triangle: Draw the base. Fold the posterboard in half along the base line. Draw a slanted line for the side. Keep the posterboard folded. Cut out the shape. Unfold.

3. Use chalk to trace the triangle on the wrong side of your fabric.

4. Cut along the chalk lines. For extra durability, either ask an adult to hem under the edges 1/4 inch or cut out your bandanna with pinking shears.

5. With the finished side of the fabric face down, fold over the base one inch. Fold it over one inch again.

6. Tie the bandanna around your pooch's neck with a double knot. Bow-wow!

Hints: Most dark-haired dogs look terrific in red. Pastels are adorable on lighter haired breeds. Denim is dandy for all dogs. Experiment with patterns: large and bold for big breeds, tiny and subtle for small. Go wild: animal prints make a fashion statement. Try polka dots for Dalmatians. Zebra stripes pop out on dogs with white or black fur. Leopard spots will bring out the beast in your canine.

Use novelty fabrics to celebrate holidays. Try black velvet or orange satin for Halloween. A green and red calico bandanna adds the finishing touch to your pet's photo with Santa. Puppy can ring in the new year with a silver or gold lamé bandanna. The possibilities are endless! Check the remnant bins in fabric stores for inspiration.

Free O' Flea Potion

Use this natural remedy to discourage fleas. Plus, your pet will smell great!

Choose one of these essential oils (available in natural food stores): bay, cedarwood, citronella, eucalyptus, lavender, orange, rose geranium, or tea tree.

Put three drops on a cotton ball. (Note: Do *not* put oil directly on your pet.) Tuck the cotton ball into the bandanna before you fold it. Refresh with oil every week.

Terrier-ific Toys

No animal is more playful with kids than the dog. Here are some simple toys you can make to amuse your pooch.

Stuff a tennis ball in a long sock, then tie a knot above the ball. You can use it for retrieving and tug-of-war games.

Deflate an old soccer ball or football enough so your dog can easily grab it. Let the games begin!

All dogs enjoy tossing and snuggling with stuffed toys. And this **Sweet Dreams Heart** will be a pup-ular plaything.

Sweet Dreams Heart

Materials:

Paper bag
Pencil
Polarfleece fabric
Needle
Pins
Thread
Scissors
Fiberfill stuffing

1. Cut open the paper bag along the sides and bottom. Spread it out flat. Draw a heart shape a little larger than you want the size of the toy. Cut out the heart.

2. Fold the fabric in half so the finished, printed sides are together with the unfinished sides on the outside.

3. Pin the paper heart pattern to the fabric. Cut along the heart outline through both pieces of fabric.

4. Thread your needle. Knot the end of the thread.

5. Use a running stitch. Stitch 1/4 inch in from the edge of the fabric. Each stitch should be about 1/8 inch long. Keeping the thread pulled firmly, make neat, even stitches. Leave open a three-inch space at the side of the heart.

6. Make an ending knot by sewing several stitches, one on top of the other. Let the thread loose, so it forms a loop. Weave the needle and thread through this loop. Pull the knot tight. Snip off any extra thread. Remove all pins.

7. Turn your heart right side out.

8. Stuff the fiberfill through the gap.

9. Pin the gap closed. Rethread and knot the needle. Sew along the gap, using tiny stitches. Make an ending knot.

Hurray for Holly-woof

Give your dog the "Holly-woof" star treatment. Run a lukewarm bath. Place one cup of oatmeal in a piece of muslin or in the foot of an old pair of pantyhose. Tie it up tightly. Let the oatmeal pouch soak in the bath water. Then add your dog. This treatment will soothe her skin. If she's dirty, give her a bath with doggy shampoo. Rinse and dry thoroughly.

If she's played with her new toys and you've given her the spa treatment, your pooch should be feeling dog-tired by now. Before nap time, why not read her a pup-ular story—one with a canine hero, of course. Tuck her in with her favorite blanket and toy. Put on some soothing classical music so she'll drift off to dreamland.

It's a dog's life!

FUN FACT: Variations in the size of dogs are enormous, with the largest dwarfing the smallest by more than 350 times!

Acquiring a dog may be the only opportunity a human ever has to choose a relative.
—Mordecai Siegal

FUN FACT: Of the 148 breeds of dogs recognized by the American Kennel Club, only ten originated in the United States. These patriotic dogs are the Alaskan Malamute, American Eskimo Dog, American Foxhound, American Water Spaniel, American Staffordshire Terrier, Australian Shepherd, which—despite the name—developed in America, Black and Tan Coonhound, Boston Terrier, Chesapeake Bay Retriever, and Cocker Spaniel.

Seasonal Care Tips

A lifetime of love means more than just a pat on the head. It's up to you to keep your dog cozy through each season, and safe and happy during each howl-iday.

Winter

Chasing snowballs, catching snowflakes on the tongue, digging snow forts—winter is an active season for dogs. Here's some tips on how to "winterize" your slush puppy.

Keep winter walks short. Use a leash—dogs can become disoriented in the snow and sleet and get lost. Be sure your pet is comfortable. Despite fur coats, dogs can also suffer from frostbite. If his fur is not thick and insulated, buy him a warm sweater or coat. Add a pair of dog boots to his wardrobe. Or wipe with a towel to remove all ice balls and rock salt from his paws.

Don't leave your pet in the car, even for several minutes. His temperature could drop drastically, causing permanent damage or even death. Antifreeze from the car is also deadly—keep your dog away from all puddles of this sweet-smelling stuff.

Check that your pet's bed is in a warm location, away from drafts. You could add a blanket so your dog can make a nest and stay warm or buy a pet heating pad.

Spring

Your dog is nibbling his paws, rubbing his face, and furiously scratching. It's too early for insects to be driving him buggy, so what's the problem? Like humans, pets can also develop allergies. Instead of sneezing and wheezing, dogs scratch their itchy skin. Ragweed, pollen, mold, and dust can all cause your pooch to scratch out an SOS.

Before he develops bald patches, take him to the vet to get allergy-tested. Antihistamines and fish oils can successfully curb symptoms. And there are a few simple things you can do to help relieve your pet. Once a week, wash his bedding in hot water. You might try the oatmeal bath treatment from page 72.

When out walking, keep your dog away from weedy areas and freshly mowed lawns. Avoid long walks during peak pollen periods, which usually occur in the early morning.

Spring also transforms your pet into a mud puppy. Keep a dark-colored towel near your door to wipe off those muddy paws.

Here's a way to have creative fun in the mud: cast your dog's pawprint. Encourage him to make tracks in wet earth. Create a circular frame around a pawprint using a strip of cardboard about two inches wide. Fasten the cardboard with a paper clip and lightly press the frame into the ground. Then mix together a ratio of two parts plaster of Paris to five parts water. Add the plaster to the water until it is the thickness of cream. Pour the plaster mixture into the frame. Let the cast harden, which usually takes only minutes. Remove the cast from the mud, take off the frame, and then rinse the mud off the cast. You can paint the plaster surrounding the pawprint to highlight your dog's special signature.

Summer

Summer signals fun for your pooch. You're on vacation and able to spend more time together playing and walking. Maybe this is the year your dog discovers the joys of swimming. Or he might accompany you and your family to the mountains. Here's how your pooch can have a safe summer.

If you and your pet are into water sports, you might start off with a dog life preserver until he learns the doggy paddle. Introduce him to the water slowly. Let him take it at his own pace. You could support his rear until he discovers how to kick with his hind legs. Reel your water dog in before he becomes too exhausted to swim. Keep your dog away from unfenced swimming pools. Even in the shallow end, dogs can drown in a flash.

At the beach, never let him drink salt water, which will make him ill. Keep your hot dog cool by letting him relax in the shade, under an umbrella. Bring along a doggy towel for him to stretch out on. Remember that hot sand burns delicate paws. He could get sunburned, too. Try putting sunscreen on his nose and the tips of his ears. Make sure it's the waterproof kind so it doesn't get licked off!

Whether you are hiking in the mountains or playing Frisbee in a city park, always stop before your dog becomes overheated. Try to avoid exercising between 11:00 a.m. and 2:00 p.m. when it is hottest. Don't allow your dog to run on hot cement or asphalt. Mowed grass or dirt trails are ideal.

Dogs have their own built-in cooling system—evaporation through panting. Your dog also will relish a drink, so bring along a canteen of cool water. Once you're both home, a crunchy ice cube is a refreshing treat. A refreshing spritz from a squirt bottle filled with cool water will also be appreciated.

Never leave your pet in a car during the summer, even for a few minutes. Heatstroke can kill a dog quickly. Your dog could escape if you open all the car windows. And if you tie him up outside, someone could walk off with him in less than a minute. It's best to leave your pet home if you can't take him everywhere with you.

If pesky fleas are driving your dog buggy, give him a bath and follow up with Disappearing Flea Juice (page 65). Keep him groomed. You can use a special flea comb and dip it in a dish of soapy water to drown those itchy insects. This is much safer than using chemical flea controls on your pet. Vacuum your dog's living quarters and wash his bed once a week in hot water.

Is your best pal joining you on vacation? It's important that his vaccinations are up to date. Keep his ID tag on at all times. You should attach an additional barrel-type tag where you can write the information on a slip of paper and place it inside. Or use a talking ID tag that plays a recorded message. Then you can write or record the location and phone number of your vacation destination.

Before the trip, don't feed your dog. Exercise him so he will be comfortable. Give him medicine from the vet if he suffers from motion sickness. Take off his leash while in the car. Let him watch the sights from the safety of a canine seat belt or a pet carrier. Never allow him to hang his head out of an open window. He could get an eye injury this way. On the journey, make pit stops for your dog to exercise and drink bottled water. Always keep him on a leash.

If your dog can't accompany you, ask other dog lovers for recommendations about where to board or good pet sitters. Visit the kennel or have the pet-sitter visit your home beforehand. Don't make a big fuss when it's time to separate from your dog. Give him a T-shirt with your scent, his favorite toy, and his usual food. You could even send him a postcard!

Autumn

The fall is a great time to take photos of your best pal against a colorful backdrop of leaves. Follow the photography hints on page 36. Construct a fort out of fallen leaves and have a leaf fight with your dog. You can also hide old tennis balls in a leaf pile for him to find. Then put him to work: bat the balls and have your dog fetch them.

Did you know that dogs who are full grown and in good health can carry up to one-quarter of their body weight in backpacks? Select a doggy backpack in the appropriate size. Start off slowly, perhaps just packing a few Gourmutt Treats (see pages 85-86) and a small pair of water bottles. Praise that pooch for carrying his own load. If your dog is having fun, you can gradually add more items, such as a canine first aid kit (see pages 19-20) and a Frisbee that can do double-duty as a water bowl. Pack the weight evenly in his backpack. Enclose non-waterproof items in plastic bags just in case your pal decides to go wading across a stream.

Show consideration for wildlife and other hikers by keeping your dog leashed on and off the trail. Keep in mind wilderness etiquette: take only pictures, leave only footprints. Pack out or bury all doggy waste. When you get back, don't forget to check your best friend's fur for burrs, foxtails, and ticks, and his paw pads for cuts and scrapes.

Howl-idays

The holidays are wonderful times to share with your best friend. Here are some ideas to get you started.

New Year's Day Start the Yappy New Year off right by promising your dog you'll spend plenty of quality time caring for and playing with him. This is the best present ever, and it's free!

Valentine's Day Announce that your dog's stolen your heart by making him the Sweet Dreams Heart on page 71.

Or show how much you love him with a relaxing massage. You can use a cookie cutter to make heart-shaped Planet K-9 Cookies on pages 59-60. Never give chocolates to your pet—they're deadly for dogs.

Easter Skip the chocolate bunnies and marshmallow chicks. Instead, why not have your pet join you in an Easter egg hunt? His superior sense of smell could give you an advantage. Most dogs drool for hard-boiled eggs. Get the okay from your vet first.

Fourth of July This is not a dog-friendly holiday. Fireworks frighten all pets. Keep your dog safe and secure in a closed room. Turn on the radio to some soothing classical music. Walk your pet on a leash. More dogs disappear on this day than any other. If your pet escapes, follow the advice in the Lost and Found section below.

Halloween Here's another holiday centering around candy—lots of it. Don't share any candy with your pooch, they can play a nasty trick on your dog's health. Whip up some delicious doggy yummies from this book instead.

Some pets are spooked by those gremlins and goblins who keep ringing that doorbell. Put your dog in a safe room so he can't escape.

You might want to dress your dog up in one of the many pet costumes available or create your own. Take pictures or go trick-or-treating together. If it's after dark, include matching reflective strips on you and your dog's costumes. There are even glow-in-the-dark bandannas and leashes with built-in flashlights!

Be careful, though, when approaching houses. They may have dogs that are not as well trained as yours is. If you can, go with a friend so you can take turns going up to the house while one of you holds your dog back a safe distance.

Thanksgiving Show your dog how thankful you are that he's your best friend. Take a hike to enjoy the colorful leaves and crisp autumn scents. Rake up a big pile of leaves and jump on in!

Keep your dog's chompers away from all those tasty morsels. Turkey bones splinter and cause choking. Some dogs can have a severe reaction to onions. And pumpkin pie adds unhealthy calories to your dog's waist.

Christmas Make sure your pet has a quiet place to rest when he needs to take a break from the festivities. Visitors and all the excitement can wear him out!

Some pet superstores and shelters sponsor holiday photos with Santa Paws. After your furry model poses, why not shop for gifts to fill your pet's Christmas stocking? Give toys designed just for dogs. Best of all, take your pooch on a long walk so he doesn't feel neglected with all the other activities going on around your house.

Make sure your cousin doesn't try to sneak your pet some rich holiday food. Dogs' tummies are easily upset by these forbidden treats. Put all food scraps, especially bones and trimmings, in a pooch-proof garbage container.

When you trim the tree, place ornaments out of your pet's reach. Don't hang food, such as candy canes and gingerbread, on the tree—it's too tempting to your dog. Tinsel is best avoided because it is dangerous if swallowed.

Although it might look cute, don't put ribbons around your dog's neck. They could get caught on something and cause choking. If you're decorating with lights, ask an adult to use power cords that shut off electricity instantly if chewed. And make sure burning candles are away from your pet's curious nose and wagging tail.

Another hazard is plants that are poisonous: mistletoe, poinsettia, holly, and others. Place them out of your pup's reach.

Not every precious pooch is as spoiled as yours is. You can make the holidays more enjoyable for homeless dogs by donating food and toys to the local animal shelter. A gift of your time—walking and playing with caged creatures—would also be appreciated.

Lost and Found

If the unthinkable happens, and your dog disappears, don't panic. Your dog is depending on you to help find him.

It's important to immediately post signs with a description and current clear photo of your pet around the neighborhood. Write the word "REWARD" in large bold letters. Call your neighbors. Place ads in your local newspapers. Read the lost and found section. Some radio stations read lost-and-found descriptions over the air.

Call the police. Alert your vet. Contact any lost-and-found pet registry services you belong to. Be sure to visit all the shelters in your area. The staffs are often overworked and might not recognize your dog from your description. Stake out all your pet's favorite hideouts. Don't panic or give up. Your dog's life could depend upon your quick and timely actions.

FUN FACT: Smart canines can understand more than 50 words.

FUN FACT: How fast can sights and sounds travel from the eyes and ears to the brain of a four-year-old Lab like Diamond Dreamer? At a super-amazing rate of 200 miles per hour!

Dogs need to sniff the ground; it's how they keep abreast of current events. The ground is a giant dog newspaper, containing all kinds of late-breaking dog news items, which, if they are especially urgent, are often continued in the next yard.
-Dave Barry

FUN FACT: You can get answers to your pet-care questions free of charge by calling (888) 252-7387. Sponsored by the American Society for the Prevention of Cruelty to Animals, this 24-hour service provides pre-recorded information about topics ranging from aging to worms.

Starting a Dog Club

Do you have friends with dogs? If the dogs get along together, you can form a doggy play group. Try out some of the activities in this book.

You can also start a dog club. Hang up some flyers at school seeking other canine fans. At your first meeting you can exchange dog photos, vote on a name for your club, and decide what activities to focus on. Here are some ideas to get you started.

Borrow the cafeteria to whip up a batch of snacks for your chow hounds. They'll be eager to get their paws on these **Gourmutt Treats**.

Gourmutt Treats

Ingredients:

Two cups whole wheat flour
1/2 cup crunchy peanut butter
1/2 cup honey
Four tablespoons wheat germ
One large egg
1/4 cup warm water
1/2 teaspoon salt

1. Stir all the ingredients together in a large mixing bowl. If the dough becomes too stiff, add another table-spoon of warm water.

2. Sprinkle flour on a cutting board. Take a handful of dough and form it into a small ball. Then, with a rolling pin flatten the ball of dough until it is about 1/2 inch thick on the cutting board.

3. Now comes the fun part. Use a dog- or bone-shaped cookie cutter to cut out the treats. Save the scraps—roll

them out again and cut more shapes. The amount of treats will depend on the size of the cookie cutter.

4. Place the treats on a baking sheet that has been sprayed with vegetable oil. Leave one inch between each treat.

5. Have an adult help you bake the treats in a 275° oven for about 25 minutes or until golden brown.

6. Remove the treats with a spatula. Let cool for 30 minutes. Store in a container...if there are any remaining.

Bone appétit!

On a nice day, your club members can exercise their dogs in the local park. Try jogging along the trails in follow-the-leader style. Keep all dogs on leashes. Don't forget your pooper-scoopers. Let the pets set the pace. Take frequent water breaks.

Why not raise money for your club with a doggy bathathon? This can be done in an assembly line on a warm, sunny day. The first person brushes and combs the dog to remove all tangles. The second person wets the dog with lukewarm water. The third person lathers up the dog using pet shampoo. The fourth person rinses off the dog until the water runs clean. The fifth person towel dries the dog.

Dog Day Afternoon

Another way to raise money is to hold a Dog Day Afternoon in the local park. Plan this several months in advance. Select a pet-friendly location. Charge admission. Make leashes mandatory. Have water and plastic bags at the entrance. Ask pet shops to donate doggy bags.

See if the local vet and dog trainer will give presentations. Maybe the shelter or breed rescuers will want to exhibit pets for adoption.

Who else do you know who is involved with dogs? Could your groomer perform a makeover on a canine volunteer? Can someone from an obedience school judge the AKC Canine Good Citizen test? Would somebody speak about volunteering to become a "puppy raiser" of guide dogs for the blind and assistance dogs for the hearing-impaired and physically disabled? Are there dogs that could demonstrate police K-9 work, search and rescue, therapy, agility, herding, carting, sledding, or tracking?

You could sell crafts, such as the Sweet Dreams Heart on page 71 or the Bow-Wow Bandannas on pages 69-70. The artist in your dog club can paint kids' faces to resemble their favorite dog breeds.

Bake batches of Gourmutt Treats to sell. Wrap up each treat in colored foil along with a "Fido's Fortune." This can be a clever saying that you print on a slip of paper. Here are a few to get you started: "A treat a day keeps the vet away." "Make no bones about it—I'm special." "Help! I'm trapped in a dog suit!" "Never let a cat get your tongue." "Just chew it!" "Every dog has his day."

Dogs can play some team games such as the canine contests on pages 40-41. Or you can set up a doggy relay race using tennis balls or sticks. Each team member must drop the ball or stick so the next member can pick it up and continue the race.

Keep up the fun with a game of follow-the-leader. The lead dog can be prompted to carry out basic commands—others in line must follow. Or why not try tug-of-war between two teams? Use a long cotton rope. Each team should have a balanced mixture of large, medium, and small dogs.

Here's a match guaranteed to bring howls of laughter— and great photos. Invite all to join in the pooches and their persons' ice cream eating competition. No hands or paws allowed—only tongues!

Hold an art contest for kids and dogs. Ask kids to draw their pets' portraits. Then send out a call for creative dogs.

Set out trays of finger-paint and rolls of butcher paper so the pooches can "paw-paint." Have jugs of water and paper towels available for clean up.

Another fun activity for the afternoon is a pet parade. Put up a sign announcing "Strut Your Mutt." Award prizes in many categories: biggest dog, smallest, fastest, slowest, smartest, silliest, loudest bark, quietest, most hair, shortest legs, best trick, longest tongue, most obedient, waggingest tail, looks most like human companion. Every dog is a winner!

Don't forget to contact your local newspaper at least two weeks before your event. This way it will receive free publicity in the calendar section. Maybe a photographer will cover the event. Or you can be a photo hound by snapping plenty of pictures and sending them to the paper's feature section. Hint: Carry a small notepad to write down people's and pets' names.

Your dog club might consider donating a portion of profits to a local humane society. Here homeless dogs of every imaginable description are searching for a new leash on life. If you can't adopt a furry friend, you can still make a difference for dogs awaiting permanent homes. Collect treats, toys, and dog food by putting up posters and setting out decorated cardboard cartons whenever you hold an event. Spend time walking a shelter dog, while giving her the exercise and attention that she craves. That wagging tail will express just how much you are appreciated!

To make this book truly interactive, I'd love to hear about all the fun stuff you enjoy doing with your dog. Which activity is you and your dog's favorite? Send your letters and photos to:

Nancy Furstinger
HCR 1, Box 63
Margaretville, NY 12455

A Note to Parents

Kids love playing with their pet dogs, but sometimes a game of fetch brings on boredom. This book contains interactive pooch projects guaranteed to pique a kid's interest and to get their dog's tail wagging. In the process, it teaches your child how to become affectionate and responsible pet guardians.

By allowing your children to attend to a pet's needs before their own, children learn altruism. However, even the most trustworthy child needs your assistance and guidance in caring for a pet. Your family should not welcome a canine companion into your home unless everyone is prepared to offer him a lifetime of loving care.

Although it is always tempting to bring home a puppy, puppies need a great deal of time and constant care. Dogs are by nature social animals and it is cruel to take a puppy away from its brothers and sisters and then abandon it for eight or more hours during a workday. Adult dogs really do make a better choice for a busy family.

Do your homework: find out as much as you can about the breed of dog you are interested in before adopting. There are Web sites (listed in the back of this book) that can help you make choices that can fit your personality and lifestyle. Dogs are not people who can learn to adjust. The different breeds have innate qualities (such as digging or running) that have been bred into them over hundreds or even thousands of years that cannot be ignored.

Almost any breed can be great with kids if given proper socialization and training. Locate obedience classes that will allow children to participate.

Stress to your children that a dog is not a toy. Show them how to be gentle when they play with the puppy.

Don't allow children to chase, hit, or jump on a puppy. Respect the puppy's privacy when he wants to be alone at mealtime or nap time. Teasing could lead to a nip. Demonstrate the proper way to lift and hold a puppy — supporting his chest and rear end while holding him close. Teach them how to handle a dog with kindness and compassion.

Encourage all family members to read the chapter Pawsitive Obedience 101. It stresses not only some simple obedience lessons, but also family cooperation to make sure that everyone uses the same commands.

The kid-canine bond is a vital and rewarding one. When these two team up, something magical happens: they become best friends. No other animal in the world offers such companionship. The activities in this book will help your child and dog amuse each other all day while they explore the joys of an interactive relationship.

Personalized Pet Pages

My dog's name is _____

Nickname _____

Birthday or adoption anniversary _____

Male _____ Female _____

Breed _____

Color and markings _____

Special features _____

Weight _____ Height (at shoulders) _____

Greatest trick _____

Favorite treat _____

Preferred toy _____

Puppy immunization dates _____

Adult immunization dates _____

Rabies vaccination dates _____

Worming dates _____

Heartworm test dates _____

Spay/Neuter date _____

Allergies _____

Medications _____

Special diet _____

Important Phone Numbers

Trainer's phone number _____

Groomer's phone number _____

Kennel's phone number _____

Pet-sitter's phone number _____

Radio station lost & found number _____

Dog warden's phone number _____

Animal shelter's phone number _____

Vet's phone number _____

Vet's emergency (weekend) number _____

Here is a photo of my dog:

Here is a lock of my dog's fur:

Here is my dog's pawprint:

Further Reading & Information

Angel Animals: Exploring Our Spiritual Connection with Animals by
Allen J. and Linda C. Anderson. Dutton/Plume, 1999.
Animal Talk: Interspecies Telepathic Communication by Penelope
Smith. Beyond Words Publishing, Inc., 1999.
ASPCA Pet Care Guide for Kids: Puppy by Mark Evans. Dorling
Kindersley, Inc., 1992.
*Best Junior Handler! A Guide to Showing Successfully in Junior
Showmanship* by Denise and Anne Olejniczak. Doral Publishing,
Inc., 1997.
Biscuits in the Cupboard by Barbara Nichol, illustrated by Philippe
Beha. Stoddart Kids, 1998.
Cool Mutts edited by J.C. Suarés. Welcome Enterprises, Inc., 1997.
Creative Crafts for Critters by Nancy Furstinger, illustrated by
Philippe Beha. Stoddart Kids, 2000.
Dr. Pitcairn's Complete Guide to Natural Health for Dogs & Cats by
Richard H. and Susan H. Pitcairn. Rodale Press, 1995.
How to Be Your Dog's Best Friend by The Monks of New Skete. Little,
Brown and Company, 1978.
How to Talk to Your Dog by Jean Craighead George, illustrated by Sue
Truesdell. Harper Collins Publishers, 2000.
James Herriot's Favorite Dog Stories by James Herriot, illustrated by
Lesley Holmes. St. Martin's Press, 1995.
Just Mutts by Steve Smith and Gene Hill. Willow Creek Press, 1996.
Lassie Come-Home by Rosemary Wells, illustrated by Susan Jeffers.
Henry Holt and Company, 1995.
*Lost and Found: Dogs, Cats, and Everyday Heroes at a Country Animal
Shelter* by Elizabeth Hess. Harcourt Brace & Company, 1998.
Scruffy by Jack Stoneley. Bullseye Books, Alfred A. Knopf, 1978.
The Tellington Touch for Dogs and Puppies by Linda Tellington-Jones
and Robyn Hood. Thane Marketing International, 1994.
The Compassion of Animals by Kristin von Kreisler. Prima
Publishing, 1997.
White Wolf: Living with an Arctic Legend by Jim Brandenburg.
Creative Publishing International, 1990.
William Wegman Puppies by William Wegman. Disney Press, 1997.

Web Sites

All About Dogs - http://dogs.about.com/pets/dogs/mbody.htm
All About Pets - http://www.petstation.com
Animal Healthcare - http://www.vetcentric.com
Animal Planet - http://animal.discovery.com
Artist Bob Ebdon's Gallery - http://www.proweb.co.uk/-bobebdon
Breed Rescue Network - http://www.prodogs.com/brn/index.htm
Canine Info - http://www.thepoop.com
Choosing the Best Dog for You - http://www.glowdog.com/bestdog
    - http://www.purina.com/dogs/index.html.
Dog Clubs - http://www.dogbiz.com/dog-clubs-usa
Doral Publishing - http://www.doralpub.com
Extensive Dog Info - http://www.dog.com
Famous Dogs - http://www.citizenlunchbox.com/famous/dogs.html
Fun with Your Dog - http://www.dog-play.com
How to Love Your Dog - http://www.geocities.com/-kidsanddogs
Information and Articles - http://www.allpets.com
Intelligence Ranking of Dog Breeds - http://www.petrix.com/dogint
    /intelligence.html
Junior Dog Lovers - http://puffin.ptialaska.net/youngs/dogs.htm
Kids and Dogs - http://www.dog-play.com/youth.html
Kids Becoming Vets - http://lam.vet.uga.edu/kids/default.html
Kids' and Dogs' Spot - http://www.workingdogweb.com
    /kids&dogs.htm
Links for Sites About Dogs - http://www.allaboutdogs.com
Older Dogs - http://www.srdogs.com
Pet Channel - http://www.thepetchannel.com
Pet Family Info - http://www.petplanet.com
Pet Horoscopes - http://www.thepetchannel.com/Horoscopes
    /index.html
Pets & Animals - http://disney.go.com/home/channels/animals
    /today/flash/index.html
Playground for Pet Lovers - http://www.doghause.com
Puppy Cam - http://www.thepuppycam.com
Rainbow Bridge - http://rainbowbridge.tierranet.com/bridge.htm
The Deaf Dog Education Action Fund - http://www.deafdogs.org
The Dog Patch - http://www.dogpatch.org
The Joy of Mutts - http://www.geocities.com/Heartland/Hills/544

Index

A

allergy, allergies, 17, 75, 76, 91
American Kennel Club (AKC),
    14, 28, 87
Autumn, 78

B

bandanna, 69, 70
birthday, 7, 59, 60, 91
Bow-Wow Bandanna, 69
breed, 11, 13, 14, 15, 17, 33, 39,
    43, 86, 89, 91, 94
breeds, 11, 12, 13, 14, 15, 18,
    70, 87, 89, 94

C

cake, 61
cavemen, 11
Christmas, 81
club, 85, 86
command, 24, 25, 26, 27, 28,
    44, 46, 50, 51
commands, 12, 23, 24, 27, 35,
    87, 90
cookie, 59, 80, 85, 86

D

Disappearing Flea Juice, 65, 78
dog club, 85, 87, 88

E

ears, 11, 20, 21, 34, 64, 66, 77
Easter, 80

F

first aid kit, 19, 79

fleas, 21, 64, 65, 70, 78
Flyball, 43, 45, 46
Fourth of July, 80
Free O' Flea Potion, 70
Frisbee, 7, 13, 43, 44, 77, 79

G

game, 9, 14, 15, 32, 39, 40, 43,
    45, 50, 60, 87, 89
games, 9, 23, 39, 60, 70, 87
Good Citizen Test, 28, 87
Gourmutt Treats, 79, 85, 87

H

Halloween, 70, 80
Herding breeds, 15
holidays, 70, 79, 82
Hound breeds, 14
hound, 60, 63, 64, 88
hounds, 14, 20, 31, 34, 59, 85

L

lost and found, 80, 82, 93
lost, 19, 20, 75, 82, 91

M

massage, 34, 64, 67, 80
mongrel, 15, 32
movie, 32
mutt, 15, 31, 33, 34, 63, 88, 93,
    94

N

nails, 63, 66
New Year's, 70, 79
No-Bake Rover Cake, 60

Non-sporting breeds, 15

O

oatmeal, 72, 76
obedience, 12, 13, 23, 24, 28,
  35, 87, 89, 90
obstacle course, 39
obstacle, 51
obstacles, 39

P

Pet Portrait Magnet, 36, 37
pet, 36, 37, 91, 93, 94
pets, 11, 12, 15, 20, 31, 35, 60,
  63, 66, 75, 80, 86, 87, 88, 94
photography, 78
photo, photos, 20, 36, 60, 70,
  78, 80, 82, 84, 87, 88, 92
Planet K-9 Cookies, 59, 61, 80
puppies, 11, 21, 27, 89
puppy, 12, 17, 18, 20, 24, 26, 27,
  28, 31, 61, 75, 76, 87, 89, 90

S

skunk, 65
Sporting breeds, 14
sports, 43, 77
Spring, 75, 76
Summer, 76
Sweet Dreams Heart, 71, 79, 87

T

tail, 7, 9, 11, 20, 21, 31, 32, 39,
  41, 49, 50, 63, 81, 88, 89
teeth, 11, 21, 63, 66, 67
Terrier, 7, 15, 33, 70
Terriers, 14, 15, 40
test, 7, 9, 13, 50, 55, 56, 87, 91
Thanksgiving, 81
ticks, 7, 79
Toy breeds, 15
toys, 15, 18, 19, 23, 24, 25, 36,

40, 44, 46, 67, 70, 71, 72, 78,
  81, 82, 88, 89, 91
trainer, 28, 86
treat, treats, 18, 24, 25, 26, 27,
  28, 40, 44, 50, 51, 52, 55, 67,
  77, 81, 85, 86, 87, 88, 91
trick, 36, 49, 50, 51, 52, 80, 88,
  91

V

Valentine's Day, 79
vet, veterinarian, 9, 17, 18, 19,
  20, 33, 43, 76, 78, 80, 82, 86,
  87, 94
video, 32

W

Web sites, 13, 89
Winter, 75
wolf, 11, 12, 18
Working breeds, 14